Indigenous Peoples' Contributions to Canada

INDIGENOUS PEOPLES IN ARTS AND MUSIC

TRUE NORTH

BY ERIN NICKS

True North is published by Beech Street Books
27 Stewart Rd. Collingwood, ON Canada L9Y 4M7

www.beechstreetbooks.ca

Produced by Red Line Editorial

Photographs ©: jamesvancouver/iStockphoto, cover, 1; Adrian Wyld/The Canadian Press/AP Images, 4–5; bigworld/iStockphoto, 7; Peter Horree/Alamy, 8–9; rook76/Shutterstock Images, 10; Ray Mickshaw/WireImage/Getty Images, 12–13; Wenn Ltd/Alamy, 14; Mark Horton/WireImage/Getty Images, 15; David Hou/Red Sky Performance, 16–17; J Morc/Shutterstock Images, 19; Sean Kilpatrick/The Canadian Press/AP Images, 20

Editor: Alyssa Krekelberg
Designer: Laura Polzin
Content Consultant: Elaine Keillor, C.M.

Library and Archives Canada Cataloguing in Publication

Nicks, Erin, author
    Indigenous peoples in arts and music / by Erin Nicks.

(Indigenous peoples' contributions to Canada)
Includes bibliographical references and index.
Issued in print and electronic formats.
ISBN 978-1-77308-348-3 (hardcover).--ISBN 978-1-77308-378-0 (softcover).--
ISBN 978-1-77308-408-4 (PDF).--ISBN 978-1-77308-438-1 (HTML)

    1. Native arts--Canada--Juvenile literature. 2. Native artists--Canada--Juvenile literature. 3. Native peoples--Canada--Music--Juvenile literature.
4. Native musicians--Canada--Juvenile literature. I. Title.

E98.A73N53 2018   j704.03'97071   C2018-902895-5
                                               C2018-902896-3

Printed in the United States of America
Mankato, MN
August 2018

TABLE OF CONTENTS

Chapter One

SCULPTURE AND MEMORIAL POLES

Indigenous Peoples contribute different forms of art to Canadian culture. Inuit have been making art for thousands of years. They are best known for carving sculptures. The sculptures can be carved out of ivory or animal bone. Limestone, marble, and other types of rock are also used for carving. Carvings can be done from whatever local stone is available. But one of the most popular types of rock used is soapstone because it is very soft. This makes soapstone easy to carve.

Inuit often carve the animals they see around them. These include polar bears, walruses, seals, owls, and fish. Each carving is a little bit different, just like the animals in the wild. Carving is a way for Inuit to explain their history.

Inuit artist Archie Ishulutak spent three days carving a sculpture of a hunter.

Carvings show how Inuit lived among Arctic animals. All animals hold important meaning for them.

INUKSHUK ART

Inuit use stones for other art, as well. Inukshuks, or inuksuit, are carefully piled rocks. They are used to help people find their way in the frozen Arctic. Inukshuks could point a person in the direction of a good hunting area. They are also used to mark **sacred** areas of land. The inukshuk has become a popular symbol for Inuit culture and art.

Sometimes stones are piled up to look like a person. This is called an inunnguaq. This means "pretend person." It also means "something that looks like a person." An inunnguaq is found on the front of the Nunavut flag. Carved inunnguaqs are sold across Canada in tourist shops. They are carved from rocks.

MEMORIAL POLE–RAISING CEREMONY

The memorial pole–raising ceremony is an important event for First Nations people on the West Coast. First they dig a hole for the pole. Many people carry the pole to the site. Then they raise it by pulling on long ropes. People dance and sing. Then the owner of the pole explains the meaning of each carving.

MEMORIAL POLES

Memorial poles are another example of Indigenous art. Memorial poles are sometimes referred to in English as totem poles. A memorial pole is a carving made out of a tall tree, such as a **cedar**. Faces and animals are carved into it from top

One of Neel's carvings is in Stanley Park, Vancouver. Neel completed this carving in 1955.

to bottom. These are called crests. Each crest belongs to a certain family or clan. Some of the most popular crests are of eagles, bears, wolves, and **thunderbirds**. The order of the crests tells the story of a family or clan. The story is often about an important event.

Ellen Neel was the first woman to become famous for carving these poles. She was born in 1916 in Alert Bay, British Columbia. She died in 1966. Her Indigenous name was Kakaso'las. This means "People Who Come to Seek Her Advice." She was of Kwakwaka'wakw heritage. She was best known for her Totemland Pole design. These carvings have a thunderbird. They also have a kneeling person carved on the bottom. Her poles can be found all over British Columbia.

Chapter Two

PAINTING AND PAINTERS

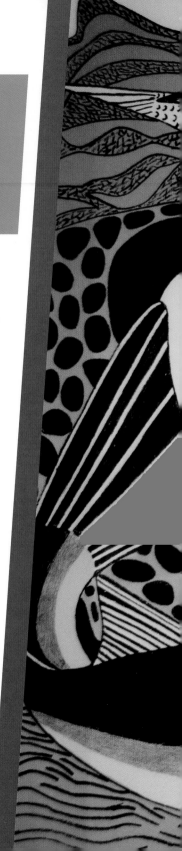

Indigenous painters can be found all over Canada. Inuit, First Nations, and Métis have different painting styles. But most like to show animals, nature, and people in their paintings.

In the 1970s several First Nations artists joined together to show their paintings. The group became known as the Professional Native Indian Artists Incorporation. Members of the group included Jackson Beardy, Eddy Cobiness, Alex Janvier, Norval Morrisseau, Daphne Odjig, Carl Ray, and Joseph Sanchez. Many of them painted in a style called woodland. Woodland art mixes animals and people into one being. For example, Morrisseau and Odjig each painted a man-and-thunderbird combination.

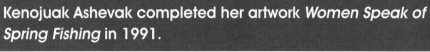

Kenojuak Ashevak completed her artwork *Women Speak of Spring Fishing* in 1991.

Centennial of the Northwest Territories 1970
Le Centenaire des Territoires du Nord-Ouest 1970

Canada 6

Inuit paintings are often made into **prints**. Prints can be made from paint or **stencils**. Prints are an easy way for Inuit to make several different versions of their art. Kenojuak Ashevak of Cape Dorset made a famous print. It is called *The Enchanted Owl*. It was printed in 1960 and appeared on a stamp in 1970. The stamp celebrated the **centennial** of the Northwest Territories.

BEADWORK AND PAINTING

Métis artists are known for their **beadwork**. Artists such as Christi Belcourt have taken the beadwork style and used it in paintings. Métis style often uses a black background. Artists create colourful designs on top of the background. Many artists like to make beadwork that looks like flowers and plants. Belcourt places tiny dots of paint on her canvas to look like beads.

Belcourt also helped design the medals for the 2015 Pan American Games. This event was held in Toronto, Ontario. Her medals were the first to include **braille**. The braille allowed blind athletes to read the words *Toronto 2015* on the medals they won.

Jane Ash Poitras is a Cree painter. She is from Fort Chipewyan, Alberta. She was born in 1951. Poitras likes to use collage in her artwork. Collage is a combination of items such as paper, fabric, or photos fitted into a new form. Poitras's paintings are easily identified by the bright colours and collages she uses.

Carl Beam was born in 1943 on Manitoulin Island, Ontario, on the M'Chigeeng First Nation. In 1985 Beam made a painting called *The North American Iceberg*. The National Gallery of Canada bought it one year later. His painting was the first work by an Indigenous artist the National Gallery of Canada purchased. Beam liked to use mixed media in his artwork. This means his paintings could include old pictures, pieces of writing, and even photos of himself.

PAINTING MASKS

First Nations artist Andy Everson wanted to combine Indigenous art and the famous masks from the Star Wars film series. He decided to paint the masks with Indigenous designs. He covered the villain's mask in black raven designs. He also painted a stormtrooper helmet and outfit with the design of a great blue heron. Stormtroopers are soldiers in Star Wars. Everson hopes his work will make people appreciate Northwest Coast history and art.

Chapter Three

INDIGENOUS MOVIES

Documentaries, dramas, and animation movies made by Indigenous filmmakers have won lots of awards. Zacharias Kunuk was born in 1957 in Nunavut. He directed *Atanarjuat (The Fast Runner)*, which is his best-known movie. It was released in 2001. It was the first feature film to be written, produced, directed, and performed in Inuktitut, the Inuit language. The movie is based on an ancient Inuit tale. The tale is about an evil spirit doing harm in the community. One warrior battles against that danger. The movie won the Caméra d'Or at the Cannes Film Festival. It also won five Genie Awards, including Best Motion Picture. The Genie Awards acknowledge great Canadian films. In 2015 it made the Top 10 Canadian Films of All Time.

Zacharias Kunuk, *right*, worked with Norman Cohn, *left*, on *Atanarjuat (The Fast Runner)*. Cohn was the director of photography.

It was ranked No. 1 by a poll held by the Toronto International Film Festival.

INDIGENOUS PEOPLES AND FILM

Many films use written versions of oral stories handed down for hundreds of years. But modern writers include Pauline Johnson, Tomson Highway, Rita Joe, Basil Johnston, Lenore Keeshig, James Bartleman, Thomas King, Drew Hayden Taylor, Armand Ruffo, and Marilyn Dumont. These award-winning writers produce poems, short stories, novels, and plays.

The Giant is an animated short film from 1987. It tells people about Edouard Beaupré. He was a Métis man born in 1881 just south of Moose Jaw, Saskatchewan. Beaupré was 2.5 metres tall. He died while he was at the 1904 World's Fair in Saint Louis, Missouri, in the United States.

Alethea Arnaquq-Baril directed *Angry Inuk*. She received a Meritorious Service Cross in 2017 for her work.

Angry Inuk is an Inuit documentary. It was released in 2016. It explains how **anti-sealing** has hurt Arctic communities. Inuit depend on seals for their meat and fur to survive. However, many people outside the Arctic do not want the seals to be killed. It is hard for outsiders to understand how important the seals are to Inuit. The movie won the People's Choice Award from Canada's Top Ten Film Festival in 2017.

Chapter Four

TRADITIONAL AND MODERN MUSIC

Indigenous languages do not have a word that is equivalent to the English word *music*. Indigenous Peoples consider producing sound an essential way to communicate with others and nature. They also consider it a way to tell stories and to produce personal healing.

For hundreds of years Indigenous Peoples have held gatherings to participate in singing and dancing. Instruments made of locally available materials include rattlers or drums. Among cultures located in southern Canada, a popular modern form of gathering is the **powwow**. At a powwow, the main music and singing is provided usually by a group of

Based in Toronto, Red Sky Performance presents dance-based theatrical productions about Indigenous subjects on stages around the world.

men, either using individual hand-held drums or seated around a large drum, which represents Earth and the **circle of life**.

Métis artists use **fiddles** to make their music. Sometimes they also use drums. The Métis learned how to play the fiddle from Irish and Scottish immigrants.

Fiddle playing is used during dancing. Métis like to do a dance called **jigging**. The fiddle music tells the dancers how fast or slow to dance.

FAMOUS MUSICAL ARTISTS

Indigenous musical artists have won many awards. Traditional Inuit throat singer Tanya Tagaq combines her singing with electronic, classical, and punk music. Tagaq won the Polaris Music Prize in 2014 for her album *Animism*.

First Nations guitarist Robbie Robertson is world famous for his time with The Band. This was a Canadian-American rock band. It was popular throughout the late 1960s and into the 1970s. The Band is in the Canadian Music Hall of Fame. It is also in the Rock and Roll Hall of Fame. In 2015 *Rolling Stone* magazine ranked Robertson 59th on its list of the 100 greatest guitarists. *Rolling Stone* publishes information on music.

TRADITIONAL AND COMPETITIVE POWWOWS

Powwows can be traditional or competitive. Traditional powwows are held within Indigenous communities. They do not have dance and drum group competitions. Competitive powwows can be large events. They have dance categories for women, men, and children. Dancers who score the highest in their category can win awards.

Tanya Tagaq grew up in Nunavut.

Buffy Sainte-Marie was the first Indigenous person to be awarded an Oscar.

Cree-Métis rapper Joey Stylez had his first big moment of fame when he opened for rapper 50 Cent in Saskatoon, Saskatchewan, in 2004. Stylez released his first album, *The Black Star*, in 2009. It received a Juno nomination.

Juno Awards recognize outstanding music. The album also got three Aboriginal Peoples' Choice Awards. In 2013 Stylez was listed as one of the top 25 best rappers in Canada by the Canadian Broadcasting Corporation. Some of Stylez's rap songs include elements of Cree singing. His Indigenous name is Grey Owl.

Singer Buffy Sainte-Marie has been making music since she was three years old. She was born in 1941 in the Piapot Cree First Nation community. This is in the Qu'Appelle Valley of Saskatchewan. She released her first album in 1964. It is called *It's My Way!* Sainte-Marie wanted to make her Indigenous heritage a part of everything she did. Her work made it easier for other Indigenous artists to break into mainstream music. Sainte-Marie's songs were popular. Her songs were often sung by other famous artists. Elvis Presley and Barbra Streisand are among the many artists who have performed her songs. Sainte-Marie's biggest artistic award came in 1982. She won an Academy Award for the song "Up Where We Belong." Academy Awards are only given to the best artists.

In addition, Indigenous musicians such as composer and conductor Andrew Balfour, cellist Cris Derksen, and operatic tenor Jeremy Dutcher participate and contribute to many kinds of music-making in Canada.

INQUIRY QUESTIONS

Why do you think it is important for Indigenous Peoples to express their cultures through different art forms? What can a non-Indigenous person learn about Indigenous cultures through art?

GLOSSARY

ANTI-SEALING
against killing seals for their fur and meat

BEADWORK
stringing beads together with a needle and thread and then sewing them to cloth

BRAILLE
a written language for blind people that uses raised dots

CEDAR
a common type of tree with very strong wood found in British Columbia

CENTENNIAL
an anniversary celebrating 100 years

CIRCLE OF LIFE
the way everything on Earth is connected

FIDDLES
musical instruments also known as violins

JIGGING
a Métis dance that is believed to have started in the 1800s from Irish and Scottish jigs

POWWOW
a celebration with traditional music and dancing

PRINTS
ink or paint placed on a roller or block and pressed onto paper

SACRED
important because it holds religious meaning

STENCILS
thin sheets of paper with cutout designs that the artist colours in with paint

THUNDERBIRDS
mythical creatures that cause thunder and lightning

TO LEARN MORE

BOOKS

Laine, Carolee. *Cree Community*. Collingwood, ON: Beech Street Books, 2017.

Murray, Laura K. *Métis Community*. Collingwood, ON: Beech Street Books, 2017.

Seigel, Rachel. *Inuit Community*. Collingwood, ON: Beech Street Books, 2018.

WEBSITES

NATIVE DANCE
art1.beechstreetbooks.ca

NATIVE DRUMS
art2.beechstreetbooks.ca

ON THE PATH OF THE ELDERS
art3.beechstreetbooks.ca

INDEX

ABOUT THE AUTHOR

Erin Nicks is from Thunder Bay, Ontario. She has worked as a writer, newspaper columnist, and reporter for nearly 20 years. She currently resides in Ottawa, Ontario.